PENGUIN PASSNOTES

GCSE Chemistry: A Book of Revision Tests

Richard Walker, B.Sc., C.Chem., MRSC, studied industrial chemistry at Loughborough University of Technology and obtained a Postgraduate Certificate in Education from Goldsmiths' College, University of London. He is currently Head of Chemistry at St Paul's Girls' School in London. He is also a course work moderator and examiner for a major examination board.

GW00645320

PENGUIN PASSNOTES

GCSE Chemistry:
A Book of Revision Tests

RICHARD WALKER, B.Sc., C.Chem., MRSC
ADVISORY EDITOR: STEPHEN COOTE, M.A., Ph.D.

PENGUIN BOOKS

PENGUIN BOOKS

Published by the Penguin Group
27 Wrights Lane, London W8 5TZ, England
Viking Penguin Inc., 40 West 23rd Street, New York, New York 10010, USA
Penguin Books Australia Ltd, Ringwood, Victoria, Australia
Penguin Books Canada Ltd, 2801 John Street, Markham, Ontario, Canada L3R 1B4
Penguin Books (NZ) Ltd, 182–190 Wairau Road, Auckland 10, New Zealand

Penguin Books Ltd, Registered Offices: Harmondsworth, Middlesex, England

First published 1988

Filmset in CRTronic Times by
EJS Chemical Composition, Bath

Made and printed in Great Britain by
Richard Clay (The Chaucer Press) Ltd,
Bungay, Suffolk

Contents

Introduction

Chemistry Revision Tests for GCSE consists of five timed tests and three multiple choice tests. Worked answers and a marking allocation are given for each question. Use the revision tests as part of your revision programme and the multiple choice tests after you are familiar with all your syllabus.

The Examination

The examination you will sit depends on your examination board. In general, however, if you are aiming for grades A–C, you will sit two papers (MEG has three). The second paper will be more difficult than the first. This book is written for any student who is taking a GCSE in chemistry, but it assumes that you will be taking the 'extended' paper and aiming for grades A–C. The listing overleaf gives, for each examining board, the allocation of marks for each paper in the examination, as well as for the practical work. The following abbreviations are used: MC = multiple choice (select the best answer from four or five options); Struct = structured questions (short responses written in spaces on the paper); and Free = long answers written in a question booklet.

Multiple choice questions

The type of multiple choice question varies slightly between boards, but with all the boards there is one mark for a correct answer: incorrect and unanswered questions get no marks. You should make sure that you answer every question. Someone knowing no chemistry at all would probably get one in five questions correct by guessing. With a small amount of knowledge, you can eliminate some of the alternatives given and therefore narrow the odds of getting the answer correct. Do this with answers you are not absolutely sure of, and you may get half or more of these right.

Examination papers for each board

LEAG: Paper I MC 40%   Paper II Struct 40% (Grades C–G)
                       or
      Pract 20%   Paper III Struct/Free 40% (Grades A–D)

MEG : Paper I MC 40%   Paper II Struct 40% (Grades C–G)
       Pract 20%   Optional Paper III (Grades A–B)

NEA : Paper I MC/Struct 80%   (Grades C–G)
       or   Pract 20%
       Paper I MC/Struct 30%   Paper II Struct/Free 50%
                                        (Grades A–B)

SEG : Paper I MC/Struct 80%   (Grades C–G)
       or   Pract 20%
       Paper II Struct 40%/Free 40% (Grades A–G)

WJEC: Paper I MC/Struct 80%   (Grades C–G)
       or   Pract: assess 10%, written 10%
       Paper I MC/Struct 40%   Paper II Struct/Free 40%
                                        (Grades A–C)

Structured questions

These require concise and clear answers. It is very easy to misread the question and include information not required, which wastes valuable time. Often, the questions follow some data or a description of an experiment. It is essential to read these introductions very carefully: the answers may well be hidden in the question.

Free response questions

These are the questions for which you are expected to plan and organize your answer. The answer you give may be quite long, and you may need to include a diagram. You are often required to choose the question from a group of three of four. Take time over this choice and don't just answer the question on a favourite topic. Other questions on unfamiliar or seemingly difficult work may be easier. Five minutes spent in selecting your question will probably be worth more to you in marks than five minutes spent answering a less suitable question.

Free response questions allow you to show off your knowledge and understanding, but it is still essential that you read the question very carefully. It is a good rule to re-read the question when you are half way through your answer. It is surprisingly easy to wander off the subject! Don't spend too long drawing diagrams. Scrappy diagrams lose marks, but excellent, coloured, book-quality diagrams will get no more marks than a competent, clear, *large* diagram that contains the information required.

Revision Tests

Each of the Revision Tests 1–3 covers a part of the GCSE syllabus. Revise this part and then complete the test. Revision Tests 4 and 5 include topics from the whole syllabus. It is essential that you do all the tests to time. When you have finished, mark your answers (strictly!) and then go through the work on which you scored poorly. If necessary, revise the work again and repeat the test after a few days.

You can measure your performance on each of the Revision Tests 1–5 using the following guidelines.

Part A: A score below half of the available marks indicates that you need to concentrate on some learning in this section.

Part B: A score above three-quarters of the available marks indicates that you have a thorough understanding of this topic; below half marks indicates that you must read through the topic again. Try to identify the parts you find difficult.

Part C: More than 15 correct answers should be sufficient for a very high grade; between 10 and 15 indicates a moderate grade. Read through the answers and work out where you went wrong. Leave the test for a day or so and then repeat it.

Part D: Below half marks indicates that you need to learn your work a little more thoroughly, but check that you have read each question carefully enough and kept to the question in your answer.

A rough guide to your overall score on each test is as follows:

More than 70%: excellent
More than 50%: average
Less than 50% : unsatisfactory.

The three multiple choice tests that follow the revision tests cover the whole syllabus and must be attempted only when you have revised all your work. If you are aiming for a Grade A or B, then you should score at least 15 in each of these tests.

Chemistry Revision Tests for GCSE covers the syllabuses of all the GCSE boards and is the companion volume to *Passnotes: Chemistry.*

Examination Boards

MEG: c/o West Midlands Examinations Board, Norfolk House, Smallbrook Queensway, Birmingham B5 4NJ.

NEA: c/o Joint Matriculation Board, Manchester M15 6EU.

LEAG: c/o London Regional Examining Board, Lyon House, 104 Wandsworth High Street, London SW18 4LF.

SEG: c/o The Associated Examining Board, Stag Hill House, Guildford, Surrey GU2 5XJ.

WJEC: c/o 245 Western Avenue, Cardiff CF5 2YX, Wales.

Revision Test 1

Subjects tested: nature of matter; separation of mixtures; atomic structure; periodicity

Part A

(10 minutes)

Fill in the missing words.

There are . . . . . . ³ .¹ states of matter: solid, ...² *liquid,* and . . . . . . .³ *gas.* The particles in a solid are closely packed together and the only movement is . . . . . .⁴. This explains why solids have a fixed . . . . . . .⁵. The particles in a liquid have restricted movement, but they move much more than those in a solid. In a gas, the particles move . . . . . .⁶ *random* in all directions.

The particles that make up these states of matter can be atoms, molecules or ions. Molecules are composed of atoms . . . . . .⁷ together. If a substance is made up of free atoms moving randomly, then the substance could be a . . . . . .⁸ gas. If the substance consists of molecules moving randomly, then it could be a . . . . . .⁹. Solid sulphur consists of . . . . . .¹⁰ moving by . . . . . .¹¹ only. Sodium chloride consists of . . . . . .¹² in fixed positions. The structure is known as an . . . . . .¹³ . . . . . .¹⁴. [½ mark each]

Total ☐

Maximum Total 7

Part B

(10 minutes)

Read the following passage and then answer the questions that follow.

The Periodic Table

In 1869 Mendeleev published his 'Periodic Law' and demonstrated that the elements, when arranged in increasing relative atomic mass, showed recurring or 'periodic' properties.

The importance of his work was quickly recognized and his Periodic Table was used successfully to predict the existence of elements unknown at that time. Germanium was one of these.

It was much later that the reason for the periodic behaviour of the elements was understood. For this, the discovery of the electron provided the information required. It is the arrangement of the electrons around the nucleus of an atom that dictates the chemical properties of an element. It was shown that this arrangement of electrons followed periodic rules, hence causing the elements to have periodic properties.

1. Give an example of a property of elements that is 'periodic'.
   . . . . [1 mark]
2. Mendeleev arranged the elements in order of increasing atomic mass. How is the modern Periodic Table arranged?
   . . . . [1 mark]
3. Describe briefly how the Periodic Table could be used to predict the existence of an element (e.g. germanium), even when it has not been discovered. . . . . [2 marks]
4. How are the electrons arranged around the nuclei of the elements of the first period of the Periodic Table (Li, Be, B, C, N, O, F, Ne)?
   . . . . [2 marks]
5. The next element in the series is Na. How are the electrons arranged around the nucleus of sodium? Why is this element placed in the same group as lithium? . . . . [2 marks]
6. Why is it that elements on the left-hand side of the Periodic Table tend to form positive ions, while those on the right-hand side tend to form negative ions? . . . . [3 marks]

                                                   Total ☐
                                          Maximum Total   11

Part C

(30 minutes)

Multiple choice questions   [1 mark each]

1. Chlorine will form an ionic compound with the element which has the electronic configuration

A 2, 7 ✓
B 2, 8
C 2, 8, 1
D 2, 8, 5
E 2, 8, 6.

2. The atoms of $^{41}_{20}X$ and $^{40}_{20}Y$
   A have different numbers of protons
   B have different numbers of neutrons
   C have the same number of neutrons
   D are allotropes
   E have 41 and 40 electrons, respectively.

3. Distillation may be used for obtaining
   1 water from copper sulphate solution
   2 pure water from sea water
   3 nitrogen from liquid air
   4 iron from a mixture of iron and sulphur
      A 1, 2, 3   B 1, 3   C 2, 4   D 4   E other.

4. The number of electrons in $^{40}_{20}Ca^{2+}$ is
   A 18
   B 20
   C 22
   D 38
   E 40.

5. An atom of an element contains 5 electrons. The element is found in group
   A I
   B II
   C III
   D V
   E VII.

Questions 6–10 refer to the following elements:
   A chlorine
   B sodium
   C sulphur
   D carbon
   E iron.

6. Which is a gas at room temperature?

7.   Which has the lowest boiling point?

8.   Which has the greatest density?

9.   Which reacts violently with water?

10. Which is yellow in colour?

11. Which of the gases below would diffuse the fastest (all measured at the same temperature and pressure)?
   A   chlorine (Cl_2)
   B   oxygen (O_2)
   C   nitrogen (N_2)
   D   carbon dioxide (CO_2)
   E   sulphur dioxide (SO_2).

12. Going down a group in the Periodic Table, which of the following *always* increases?
   A   boiling point
   B   chemical reactivity
   C   melting point
   D   atom size
   E   ionization energy.

13. A certain ink was separated using chromatography. A drop of the ink was placed on a piece of filter paper together with drops of pure dyes. The chromatogram shown below was obtained. The ink contains

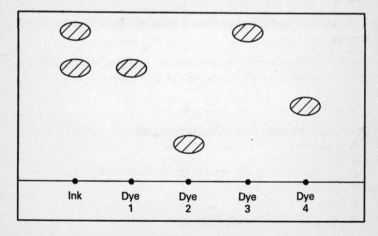

A dyes 1, 2, 3, 4
B dyes 1, 2, 3
C dyes 1, 4
D dyes 1, 2
E dyes 1, 3.

Questions 14–17 refer to the following methods of separation:
A fractional distillation
B chromatography
C filtration
D distillation
E separating funnel.

Which method is best used to separate

14. water from tap water?

15. hexane from crude oil?

16. tetrachloromethane (carbon tetrachloride) from a mixture of tetrachloromethane and water?

17. water from ink?

18. Which of the following statements about ionic compounds is incorrect?
A they are formed between metals and non-metals
B they have high melting points
C they conduct electricity in the solid state
D they are composed of positive and negative ions
E the particles in the compound can only vibrate.

19. An element has an atomic number of 12. It would be expected to have similar properties to the element of atomic number
A 2
B 3
C 4 ✓
D 5
E 6.

20. The structure of iodine crystals is best described by
A widely separated atoms
B widely separated ions
C widely separated molecules

   D closely packed molecules
   E closely packed ions.

Total ☐
Maximum Total   20

Part D

(40 minutes)

Structured questions

1. A shortened form of the Periodic Table is shown below. The atomic numbers of the elements have been included. Use only the numbers in the Periodic Table to answer the questions.

1							2
3	4	5	6	7	8	9	10
11	12	13	14	15	16	17	18

(a) What are the atomic numbers of the noble gases?
   . . . . [1 mark]

(b) What is the electronic configuration of element 11?
   . . . . [1 mark]

(c) What are the atomic numbers of the alkali metals (Li, Na) and the
halogens (F, Cl)?   . . . . [2 marks]

(d) What is the nature of the bonding (covalent or ionic) in the
compound formed between elements (i) 3 and 9 and (ii) 6 and 17.
   . . . . [2 marks]

(e) (i)   What happens to the atomic size of elements 3–10 and 11–18?
       Explain.   . . . . [2 marks]
    (ii) Give another periodic property (*not* atomic size) that is shown
       by elements 3–18. For the property you have chosen, indicate
       its trend across the period.   . . . . [2 marks]

(f) What is the formula of the chloride of elements X (atomic number
11) and Y (atomic number 14)?   . . . . [2 marks]

2. The table below gives the physical properties of some elements. The letters of the elements are not the symbols of the elements.

Elements	Melting point (°C)	Boiling point (°C)	Magnetic	Density (g cm⁻³)	pH of a solution of the oxide of the element
A	Sublimes at 3727°C		No	2.25	4
B	1410	2677	No	2.33	Insoluble
C	−220	−188	No	Very small	3
D	650	1117	Yes	1.74	10
E	98	890	Yes	0.97	14
F	−189	−186	No	Very small	No oxide formed

(a) Which of the elements are metals? Explain your choice.
.... D + E magnet C ..... [3 marks]

(b) Which of the elements are gases? Give *two* reasons for your ·choice. .......C.F...................... [3 marks]

(c) Give the letter corresponding to (i) a solid non-metal; (ii) a noble gas; and (iii) the element which is liquid over the smallest temperature range. .... [3 marks]

3. (a) What is the electronic configuration (structure) of the chlorine atom? .... [1 mark]

(b) Show, by using a diagram, the electronic structure (outer shells only) of the chlorine molecule. .... [2 marks]

(c) What is the electronic configuration (structure) of the sodium atom? .... [1 mark]

(d) When sodium reacts with chlorine, the sodium and chlorine form ions. Draw diagrams showing the electronic structure (outer shells only) of these two ions. .... [2 marks]

(e) Give *two* properties common to ionic compounds.
.... [2 marks]

Total ☐

Maximum Total 29

Answers to Revision Test 1

Part A

1. three; 2. liquid; 3. gas; 4. vibrational; 5. shape; 6. randomly;
7. bonded; 8. noble; 9. halogen (or any other molecular gas);
10. molecules; 11. vibration; 12. ions; 13. ionic; 14. lattice.

Part B

1. Ionization energy or atomic size or melting point.
2. The elements are arranged by atomic number (number of protons in nucleus).
3. The elements are arranged in sequence. If one is missing from the sequence, then its properties can be predicted by looking at the properties of the elements above and below it in the group to which it belongs. For example, Ge is below Si and above Sn: it will therefore have properties similar to these two elements.
4. Li (2, 1), Be (2, 2), B (2, 3), C (2, 4), N (2, 5), O (2, 6), F (2, 7), Ne (2, 8).
5. Na (2, 8, 1). They both have one outer electron: their properties will therefore be similar.
6. On the left-hand side of any one period, atoms have few outer electrons. These are easily removed to form positive ions because the nuclear charge is relatively small. On the right-hand side of this period, the nuclear charge is greater and extra electrons are attracted to the atoms. These atoms form negative ions.

Part C

1. C (a metal)
2. B (isotopes not allotropes!)
3. A
4. A (20 in neutral atom; ion loses 2)
5. C (electronic configuration 2, 3)
6. A
7. A (the gas)
8. E (transition metal)
9. B (alkali metal)
10. C
11. C (smallest relative molecular mass)

12. D (ionization energy, the energy to form positive ions, always decreases)
13. E
14. D
15. A
16. E (immiscible liquids)
17. D (*not* chromatography)
18. C (they conduct in the molten state)
19. C (electronic configuration 2, 8, 2, so the element is in group II)
20. D (I_2 in a lattice).

Part D

1. (a) 2, 10, 18.
    (b) 2, 8, 1.
    (c) Li = 3, Na = 11, F = 9, Cl = 17.
    (d) (i) ionic; (ii) covalent.
    (e) (i) It decreases as the nuclear charge increases, attracting the electrons with greater force.
    (ii) Ionization energy; this increases across the period.
    (f) XCl and YCl_4.

2. (a) D and E: they have high melting points; they are magnetic; and they form alkaline oxides. (There is no evidence to *confirm* that B is a metal.)
    (b) C and F: they have boiling points below 20°C and have very low densities.
    (c) (i) A; (ii) F; and (iii) F.
3. (a) 2, 8, 7.
    (b)

$$\overset{\times\ \times}{\underset{\times\ \times}{\overset{\times}{\underset{\times}{Cl}}}} \qquad \overset{\circ\ \circ}{\underset{\circ\ \circ}{\overset{}{\underset{\circ}{Cl}}}}\circ$$

    (c) 2, 8, 1.
    (d)

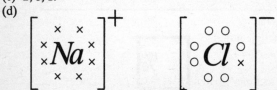

(e) They are high-melting-point solids and they conduct electricity when molten or in solution.

Score for Revision Test 1

Part A	☐
	7
Part B	☐
	11
Part C	☐
	20
Part D	☐
	29
Total	☐
	67

☐ %

Revision Test 2

Subjects tested: chemical calculations (the mole, formulae, equations) and chemical changes (heat changes, speeds of reactions); metals (extraction, reactivity)

Part A

(10 minutes)

Fill in the missing words.

Metals tend to react by . . . . . .¹ electrons. In so doing, they form
. . . . . .² ions. The compounds of metals are therefore ionic compounds
which have . . . . . .³ melting points and conduct electricity when
. . . . . .⁴ or . . . . . .⁵.

   If a molten salt of a metal is electrolysed, then the . . . . . .⁶ ions are
attracted to the negative electrode (the . . . . . .⁷), where they . . . . . .⁸
electrons to become . . . . . .⁹. This method of forming metals is used in
the extraction of . . . . . .¹⁰. In this case, the metal cannot be extracted
by electrolysing a solution of its salt or by displacement (reduction) with
. . . . . .¹¹ because it is too reactive. The latter method is used for the
extraction of . . . . . .¹². [½ mark each]

Total ☐

Maximum Total 6

Part B

(10 minutes)

Read the following passage and then answer the questions that follow.

Many substances liberate energy when they are burnt in air, although
not all substances are suitable as fuels. Petrol, which can be thought of as
octane (C_8H_{18}), gives 42 kJ for every gram, whereas hydrogen produces
143 kJ per gram when completely burnt in oxygen. It is rare for
hydrogen to be used as a fuel, however, even though it is far cleaner and
produces far less pollution than petrol when burnt. Sugar gives 17 kJ per

gram, but is never used as a fuel. Carbon in the form of coal delivers 33 kJ per gram and is a common fuel, but has some disadvantages.

1. Give two properties of a substance that make it useful as a fuel.
.... [2 marks]
2. How much heat is liberated when 1 mole of octane is completely burnt in air? .... [3 marks]
3. Hydrogen causes far less pollution than octane when burnt. Give the name of *one* possible pollutant when octane burns.
.... [1 mark]
4. Why is sugar never used as a fuel? .... [1 mark]
5. When coal burns, it delivers 33 kJ per gram. This is an average figure for all types of coal. The figure varies because of the presence of impurities in the coal. Give the names of *two* impurities in coal.

.... [2 marks]

Total ☐
Maximum Total 9

Part C

(30 minutes)

Multiple choice questions [1 mark each]

1. In an experiment, iron filings are added to silver nitrate solution. It was found that 1.4 g iron fillings displaces 5.4 g of silver from the solution. The ratio of the number of moles of iron to silver (relative atomic masses: $Fe = 56$; $Ag = 108$) is
   A 1:1
   B 1:2
   C 2:1
   D 3:1
   E 2:3.

2. Which of the following compounds contains the greatest percentage by mass of carbon?
   A methane (CH_4)
   B ethane (C_2H_6)
   C ethyne (C_2H_2)
   D butane (C_4H_{10})
   E decane ($C_{10}H_{22}$).

3. A solution of copper sulphate is electrolysed. The particles that carry electric charge through the solution are known as
   A electrons
   B neutrons   *electron through metals*
   C protons
   D atoms
   E ions. ✓

Which of the graphs A–E matches the description in questions 4–7?

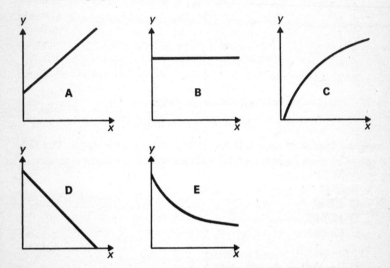

4. The mass of copper oxide in a heated crucible (*y* axis) against time (*x* axis).

5. The mass of hydrated copper sulphate in a heated crucible (*y* axis) against time (*x* axis).

6. The volume of hydrogen gas formed when a piece of magnesium is placed in dilute hydrochloric acid (*y* axis) against time (*x* axis).

7. The mass of a copper cathode during the electrolysis of copper sulphate (*y* axis) against the amount of charge passed (*x* axis).

8. In an industrial plant, metal strips immersed in an acid corrode too quickly. Which one of the following will slow the rate of corrosion?

   A heating the acid
   B increasing the concentration of the acid
   C using longer strips of metal
   D cooling the acid
   E using a more reactive metal.

9. When 2.46 g of hydrated magnesium sulphate is heated to constant weight, the residue has a mass of 1.20 g. What is the value of x in the formula $MgSO_4.xH_2O$ (relative molecular masses: $MgSO_4 = 120$; $H_2O = 18$)?

   A 1
   B 2
   C 4
   D 5
   E 7.

10. The reaction between carbon and oxygen is

$$C(s) + O_2(g) \rightarrow CO_2(g)$$

When 1 mole of carbon burns, 390 kJ of heat are evolved. The heat evolved when 2 g of carbon $(C = 12)$ are completely burnt in oxygen is

   A 32.5 kJ
   B 65 kJ
   C 195 kJ
   D 1170 kJ
   E 2340 kJ.

11. Electrolysis is used to extract
   1 copper from copper sulphide ore
   2 aluminium from aluminium oxide
   3 iron from iron oxide
   4 magnesium from magnesium oxide
   A 1, 2, 3 B 1, 3 C 2, 4 D 4 E other.

12. A metal burns in oxygen with a lilac flame. The oxide that is formed readily dissolves in water and the solution turns litmus blue. The element is most likely to be

   A chlorine
   B potassium
   C sodium
   D carbon
   E calcium.

13. Calcium carbonate is added to the blast furnace in the extraction of iron because
   A it reduces the iron oxide to iron
   B it oxidizes the carbon to carbon monoxide
   C it reacts with sand to form slag
   D it lowers the temperature of the reaction
   E it lowers the melting point of iron.

14. Which of the following is oxidation?
   A loss of protons
   B addition of electrons
   C loss of electrons
   D addition of hydrogen
   E addition of a metal.

Questions 15–18: a student studied the rate at which hydrogen gas was evolved in the reaction between magnesium and hydrochloric acid.

The solid line is the result obtained when $200 \, cm^3$ of $1.0 \, mol \, dm^{-3}$ hydrochloric acid (excess) is added to 1 g of magnesium ribbon.

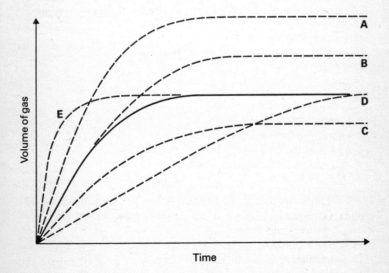

Select from the lines A–E the graph that would be obtained if

15. a more concentrated acid were used with 1.0 g of magnesium ribbon.

16. 2 g of magnesium ribbon were used with the original acid.

17. 1 g of powdered magnesium were used with the original acid.

18. 1 g of magnesium were used with the original acid, which had been cooled in a refrigerator.

19. Caesium is in group I of the Periodic Table, placed below potassium. It is likely to
   1 react with chlorine
   2 be more reactive than sodium
   3 form coloured compounds
   4 react vigorously with water
   A 1, 2, 3   B 1, 3   C 2, 4   D 4   E other.

20. Which of the following reactions is (are) exothermic?
   1 condensation of steam
   2 reaction of sodium with water
   3 melting of ice
   4 burning of carbon in air
   A 1, 2, 3   B 1, 3   C 2, 4   D 4   E other.

Total ☐
Maximum Total 20

Part D

(40 minutes)

Structured questions

1. (a) The number of particles in 1 mole of a substance is Avogadro's constant L. State, in terms of L, the number of (i) atoms in 4 g of helium (He = 4); (ii) molecules in 44 g of carbon dioxide (C = 12; O = 16); and (iii) ions in 40 g magnesium oxide (MgO: Mg = 24; O = 16). . . . . **[3 marks]**

(b) Hydrogen gas reacts with copper oxide according to the following equation:

$$CuO(s) + H_2(g) \rightarrow Cu(s) + H_2O(l)$$

(i) Calculate the mass of copper that would be produced when 4 g of copper oxide completely reacts.

. . . . [3 marks]

(ii) Calculate the mass of water that would be formed in the same reaction. [2 marks]

2. Six metals are listed below: the most reactive is on the left; the least reactive on the right.

potassium magnesium zinc copper silver

(a) Which of the metals is the most likely to tarnish rapidly in air?

. . . . [1 mark]

(b) Which of the metals will react with cold dilute acid to give hydrogen, but does not react with water? . . . . [1 mark]

(c) Which metal is most likely to be formed in nature as the pure metal? . . . . [1 mark]

(d) Which metal is most likely to be extracted using a displacement (reduction) reaction? . . . . [1 mark]

(e) What would you see happen when powdered magnesium is added to copper sulphate solution? Write a word equation for the reaction taking place. . . . . [3 marks]

(f) Which of the metals is the most powerful reducing agent?

. . . . [1 mark]

3. An experiment was performed to investigate the rate of reaction between calcium carbonate and hydrochloric acid. The volume of carbon dioxide evolved was measured with time. The following results were obtained:

Time (min)	½	1	1½	2	2½	3	3½	4	4½	5	5½	6	6½
Volume CO_2 (cm³)	24	42	56	66	75	82	87	90	93	95	96	96	96

(a) Write an equation for the reaction between calcium carbonate and hydrochloric acid. . . . . [1 mark]

(b) Plot a graph of the volume of gas against time.
. . . . [2 marks]
(c) Use the graph to answer the following questions:
    (i)   What was the total volume of gas evolved?   . . . . [1 mark]
    (ii) At what time did the reaction cease? . . . . [1 mark]
    (iii) At what time was the reaction the fastest? Give a reason for
          your answer. . . . . [2 marks]
    (iv) At what time was the reaction half complete?
. . . . [1 mark]
(d) Give *three* methods by which the rate of this reaction could be
increased. . . . . [3 marks]

Total ☐
Maximum Total 27

Answers to Revision Test 2

Part A

1. losing; 2 positive; 3. high; 4. aqueous; 5. molten; 6. positive;
7. cathode; 8. gain; 9. atoms; 10. aluminium (or any reactive metal);
11. carbon; 12. iron (or any less reactive metal).

Part B

1. Substances that burn rapidly and liberate heat in doing so make
   useful fuels.
2. 1 mole of octane (C_8H_{18}) has a mass of 114 g. Therefore, when
   1 mole of octane is burnt, $114 \times 42 = 4788$ kJ of heat are liberated.
3. Carbon monoxide.
4. Because it is difficult to start combustion.
5. Sulphur and silicates (rocks).

Part C

1. B (0.025 mole Fe : 0.05 mole Ag)
2. C (%C = 24/26 × 100 = 92%)
3. E (electrons carry charge through metals)
4. B (mass remains constant)
5. E (water of crystallization is lost)
6. C (volume increases until end of reaction)
7. A (Faraday's law)

8. D
9. E (1.26 g water = 0.07 mole from 0.01 mole of $MgSO_4$)
10. B 2 g carbon = $\frac{1}{6}$ mole; therefore $\frac{1}{6} \times 390 = 65$ kJ are evolved)
11. C (copper and iron are extracted by displacement/reduction)
12. B (solution of oxide is alkaline; this indicates metal)
13. C
14. C
15. E (same volume of gas, but faster reaction rate)
16. B (same reaction rate, but greater volume of gas)
17. E (same volume of gas, but faster reaction rate)
18. D (same volume of gas, but slower reaction rate)
19. E (1, 2, 4)
20. E (1, 2, 4)

Part D

1. (a) (i) L; (ii) L; and (iii) $2L$.
   (b) (i) 4 g CuO = 4/80 = 0.05 mole (CuO = 80); therefore
       $0.05 \times 64 = 3.2$ g of copper are produced.
       (ii) 0.05 mole H_2O = 0.05×18 = 0.9 g.

2. (a) Potassium; (b) zinc (note that Mg reacts with steam); (c) silver;
   (d) copper; (e) blue colour discharged, brown solid deposit formed,
   magnesium + copper sulphate → magnesium sulphate + copper;
   (f) potassium (most easily oxidized to ions).

3. (a) $CaCO_3(s) + 2HCl(aq) \rightarrow CaCl_2(aq) + CO_2(g) + H_2O(l)$
   (b)

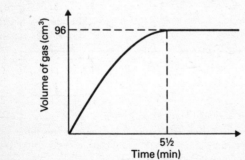

(c) (i) 96 cm³; (ii) 5½ min; (iii) at the start, because reactants are
    at their most concentrated then; and (iv) 1¼ min (it is half
    complete when half the gas has evolved, i.e. 96/2 = 48 cm³).

(d) Increase the temperature; use powdered calcium carbonate; or use more concentrated acid.

Score for Revision Test 2

Part A	☐
	6
Part B	☐
	9
Part C	☐
	20
Part D	☐
	27
Total	☐
	62

☐ %

Revision Test 3

Subjects tested: acids and bases; non-metals; organic chemistry

Part A

(10 minutes)

Fill in the missing words.

The air around us is composed of some very important gases. . . . . . . [1], which makes up about 78% of the air, is chemically . . . . [2], but can be made to react with hydrogen to form . . . . [3], which finds uses in the . . . . [4] and . . . . [5] industries. Oxygen makes up about . . . . [6]% of the air and is chemically . . . . [7]. It forms . . . . [8] with most other elements. These compounds can be either . . . . [9] bonded or . . . . [10] bonded, depending on the other element present. Carbon dioxide makes up only about 0.03% of the air. This proportion has remained roughly constant over many centuries because, although substances like . . . . [11] produce carbon dioxide when burnt, ... [12] use the carbon dioxide to produce glucose and oxygen. This reaction is known as . . . . . . [13] because . . . . . . [14] is needed for the reaction to occur.   [½ mark each]

Total ☐

Maximum Total   7

Part B

(10 minutes)

Read the following passage and then answer the questions that follow.

Over many centuries, dead and decaying animals and plants have been degraded into relatively simple organic substances trapped in the earth. Crude oil is the result of decayed microscopic organisms from the sea becoming trapped in porous rock. If the porous rock is 'capped' by impervious rock, then the crude oil will lie under pressure in the porous rock for many years until disturbed by drilling.

Crude oil is a mixture of many different compounds; the most common, by far, are the hydrocarbons. Amongst these, alkanes are the most abundant. These substances may be separated from the mixture and then chemically treated by a sequence of reactions (e.g. cracking and polymerization).

1. What is a hydrocarbon?   *Fossil Fuel* .. *hydrogen + carbon* .... [1 mark]
2. What is an alkane? Give an example of a liquid alkane found in crude oil.   .... [2 marks]
3. Above the crude oil in the porous rock is often found a gas (natural gas). Give the formula for the molecules of a substance found in this gas.   .... [1 mark]
4. What method is used to separate the alkanes from crude oil?
   .... [1 mark]
5. What are the products of cracking alkanes? Write an equation to illustrate cracking.   .... [3 marks]
6. What group of substances derived from crude oil can undergo polymerization? Write an equation to illustrate polymerization.
   .... [2 marks]

Total ☐
Maximum Total   10

Part C

(30 minutes)

Multiple choice questions   [1 mark each]

Questions 1–5 concern the following gases:
   A ammonia
   B nitrogen
   C chlorine
   D oxygen
   E carbon dioxide.

1. Which gas cannot be collected by bubbling it through water because it is so soluble?

2. Which gas turns damp litmus paper pink and then decolorizes it?

3. Which gas is odourless, colourless, non-flammable and has no effect on lime water?

4. Which gas has the greatest density?

5. Which gas makes up the largest proportion of air? *B*

6. Which of the following is a compound?
   A air
   B sulphur
   C brass ✓
   D water ✓
   E oxygen.

7. The product of the reaction between butene and bromine is

A
$$H-\underset{\underset{H}{|}}{\overset{\overset{H}{|}}{C}}-\underset{\underset{H}{|}}{\overset{\overset{H}{|}}{C}}-\underset{}{\overset{\overset{Br}{|}}{C}}=\underset{}{\overset{\overset{Br}{|}}{C}}$$

B
$$Br-\underset{\underset{Br}{|}}{\overset{\overset{Br}{|}}{C}}-\underset{\underset{Br}{|}}{\overset{\overset{Br}{|}}{C}}-\underset{\underset{Br}{|}}{\overset{\overset{Br}{|}}{C}}-\underset{\underset{Br}{|}}{\overset{\overset{Br}{|}}{C}}-Br$$

C
$$H-\underset{\underset{H}{|}}{\overset{\overset{H}{|}}{C}}-\underset{\underset{H}{|}}{\overset{\overset{H}{|}}{C}}-\underset{\underset{Br}{|}}{\overset{\overset{H}{|}}{C}}-\underset{\underset{H}{|}}{\overset{\overset{H}{|}}{C}}-H$$

D
$$H-\underset{\underset{H}{|}}{\overset{\overset{H}{|}}{C}}-\underset{\underset{H}{|}}{\overset{\overset{H}{|}}{C}}-\underset{\underset{Br}{|}}{\overset{\overset{H}{|}}{C}}-\underset{\underset{Br}{|}}{\overset{\overset{H}{|}}{C}}-H$$

E
$$H-\underset{\underset{H}{|}}{\overset{\overset{H}{|}}{C}}-\underset{\underset{H}{|}}{\overset{\overset{H}{|}}{C}}-\underset{\underset{H}{|}}{\overset{\overset{H}{|}}{C}}-\underset{\underset{H}{|}}{\overset{\overset{H}{|}}{C}}-H$$.

Questions 8–11 refers to the fractionating column overleaf. Select the most suitable answer to each question.

8. Which fraction has the lowest boiling point?

9. Which fraction could be used as a surface material for roads?

10. Which fraction is a component of Calor gas ('bottled gas')?

11. Which fraction is the fuel in a car engine?

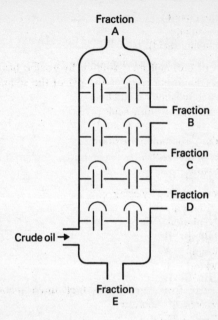

Fraction A

Fraction B

Fraction C

Fraction D

Crude oil →

Fraction E

12. Photosynthesis and respiration both
A form carbon dioxide
B use carbon dioxide
C increase the concentration of oxygen in the atmosphere
D require light energy ✓
E occur in living things.

13. The propellant gas in an aerosol is ideally insoluble in water, non-flammable and not affected by acids or alkalis. Which of the following gases would be the *most* suitable for use in an aerosol?
A carbon dioxide
B nitrogen
C propane
D ammonia
E hydrogen.

14. A sample of soil has a pH of 5. The soil may be neutralized by adding
A ammonium nitrate
B urea

C lime (calcium oxide)
D calcium phosphate
E vinegar (ethanoic acid).

15. A solution of $0.01 \, mol \, dm^{-3}$ sodium hydroxide has a pH of 13. A substance is added that changes the pH of the sodium hydroxide solution to 14. The substance could be
    A $0.1 \, mol \, dm^{-3}$ hydrochloric acid
    B water
    C $0.01 \, mol \, dm^{-3}$ sodium hydroxide
    D solid sodium hydroxide
    E carbon dioxide.

16. Starch is best detected by using
    A Fehling's solution
    B Benedict's solution
    C iodine solution
    D litmus solution
    E bromine water.

17. The molecular formulae of the first three members of the homologous series of alcohols are
    A CH_2O, CH_3O, CH_4O
    B CH_4O, C_2H_6O, C_3H_8O
    C HOH, COH, C_2OH
    D C_2H_6O, C_2H_3OH, CH_3OCH_3
    E C_2H_6O, C_3H_8O, $C_4H_{10}O$.

18. A substance is an acid if it
    A reacts with a metal oxide
    B accepts protons
    C has a sour taste
    D is corrosive
    E has a pH value of less than 7.

19. Which of the following will give a white precipitate if added to sulphuric acid?
    A silver nitrate solution
    B sodium hydroxide solution
    C barium chloride solution
    D copper nitrate solution
    E universal indicator.

20. Which one of the following oxides dissolves in water to give a solution that has a pH of less than 7?
   A aluminium oxide
   B nitrogen(II) oxide
   C sulphur dioxide
   D carbon monoxide
   E sodium oxide.

Total ☐
Maximum Total   20

Part D

(40 minutes)

Structured questions

1. Nitric acid is manufactured by oxidizing ammonia according to the equation

$$4NH_3 + 5O_2 \rightleftharpoons 6H_2O + 4NO$$

The nitrogen oxide is further oxidized to nitrogen dioxide by mixing it with air

$$4NO + 2O_2 \rightarrow 4NO_2$$

The nitrogen dioxide is dissolved in water in the presence of air

$$4NO_2 + 2H_2O + O_2 \rightarrow 4HNO_3$$

(a) Give the name of a catalyst used in the oxidation of ammonia.
. . . . [1 mark]
(b) From what raw materials is ammonia manufactured?
. . . . [2 marks]
(c) (i) Nitric acid is often used to produce ammonium nitrate. Describe how ammonium nitrate may be prepared from nitric acid. . . . . [2 marks]
   (ii) What is ammonium nitrate used as? . . . . [1 mark]
(d) 4 moles of nitric acid (relative molecular mass = 63) require 4 moles of ammonia (relative molecular mass = 17) to react. What mass of ammonia is required to manufacture 1 tonne (1000 kg) of nitric acid? . . . . [3 marks]

2. Use the substances listed in Table A to complete Table B.

Table A

Acids	Alkalis	Metals	Other
Hydrochloric acid	Sodium hydroxide	Magnesium	Copper oxide
Sulphuric acid	Potassium hydroxide	Zinc	Lead nitrate
Nitric acid	Magnesium hydroxide	Copper	Lead oxide
Ethanoic (acetic) acid			Sodium sulphate

Table B

Salt to be formed	Reactants (in words)	Products (in words)
Sodium chloride	Hydrochloric acid + sodium hydroxide	(a) . . . . .
Zinc nitrate	(b)	(c) . . . . .
Copper chloride	(d)	(e) . . . . .
Zinc sulphate	(f)	(g) . . . . .
Magnesium ethanoate	Magnesium + ethanoic acid	(h) . . . . .
Lead chloride	(i)	(j) . . . . .

[1 mark each]

3. Octane is a saturated hydrocarbon belonging to the homologous series of alkanes. When heated with a catalyst in the absence of air, octane forms two hydrocarbons with shorter carbon chain lengths. One of these is saturated, but the other is unsaturated. Answer the following questions.

(a) What is meant by **saturated**? . . . . [1 mark]
(b) What is meant by **unsaturated**? . . . . [1 mark]
(c) What name is given to the reaction by which octane forms two compounds, one of which is unsaturated? . . . . [1 mark]
(d) Give the name of a possible example of the unsaturated hydrocarbon. . . . . [1 mark]
(e) What would you *see* if this unsaturated hydrocarbon were mixed with a solution of bromine? . . . . [1 mark]

(f) With a catalyst, the unsaturated hydrocarbon reacts to form a solid substance X that becomes soft when warmed. What has been formed in this reaction?   . . . . [1 mark]

(g) Give one other physical property of X.   . . . . [1 mark]

(h) Give a possible use of X.   . . . . [1 mark]

(i) Give a possible disadvantage when using X.   . . . . . . [1 mark]

(j) What substances are formed when X burns in the air?

. . . . [1 mark]

Total ☐

Maximum Total 29

Answers to Revision Test 3

Part A

1. nitrogen; 2. inert (or unreactive); 3. ammonia; 4. fertilizer; 5. explosive; 6. 20; 7. reactive; 8. oxides; 9. ionically; 10. covalently; 11. coal (or wood etc.); 12. plants; 13. photosynthesis; 14. light.

Part B

1. A compound that contains carbon and hydrogen only (the word 'only' is important).

2. A hydrocarbon of general formula C_nH_{2n+2}; e.g. octane.

3. CH_4 or C_2H_6.

4. Fractional distillation.

5. Shorter-chain alkanes and alkenes:

6. Alkenes:

$$n\left(\begin{array}{c}H\\ \diagdown\\ H\end{array}C=C\begin{array}{c}H\\ \diagup\\ H\end{array}\right) \longrightarrow \left(\begin{array}{cccc}H&H&H&H\\ |&|&|&|\\ -C-C-C-C-\\ |&|&|&|\\ H&H&H&H\end{array}\right)_n$$

Part C

1. A (remember the fountain experiment?)
2. C (chlorine bleaches)
3. B (nitrogen is almost inert)
4. C (the greatest relative molecular mass)
5. B (80%)
6. D (brass is an alloy)
7. D (addition across the double bond)
8. A (the gases)
9. E (bitumen, tar)
10. B
11. C (fraction D would be diesel or fuel oil)
12. E
13. B
14. C (soil is acidic; lime dissolves to give calcium hydroxide)
15. D (must be made *more* alkaline)
16. C
17. B (CH_3OH, C_2H_5OH, C_3H_7OH)
18. E
19. C (insoluble barium sulphate formed)
20. C (NO and CO are neutral oxides)

Part D

1. (a) Platinum.
   (b) Air and water or methane.
   (c) (i) A solution of nitric acid is treated with ammonia solution until neutral. The ammonium nitrate is separated by evaporation; (ii) a fertilizer.
   (d) 1000 kg nitric acid = 1 000 000/63 moles.
   Therefore 17 × 1 000 000/63 = 270 kg of ammonia are required. This is 0.27 tonnes.

2. (a) Sodium chloride + water.
   (b) Zinc + nitric acid.
   (c) Zinc nitrate + hydrogen.
   (d) Copper oxide + hydrochloric acid.
   (e) Copper chloride + water.
   (f) Zinc + sulphuric acid.
   (g) Zinc sulphate + hydrogen.
   (h) Magnesium ethanoate + hydrogen.
   (i) Lead nitrate + hydrochloric acid.
   (j) Lead chloride + nitric acid.

3. (a) The compound contains single bonds.
   (b) The compound has at least one carbon to carbon double bond.
   (c) Cracking.
   (d) Ethene (or propene).
   (e) Bromine decolorized.
   (f) A polymer (or plastic).
   (g) Insulator or unreactive.
   (h) Packaging, etc.
   (i) It does not react and is therefore difficult to dispose of.
   (j) Carbon dioxide and water.

Score for Revision Test 3

Part A	7
Part B	10
Part C	20
Part D	29
Total	66

%

Revision Test 4

All syllabus topics

Part A

(10 minutes)

Fill in the missing words.

Metal elements exist as metallic lattices. The atoms are arranged in ......[1] dimensions and each atom loses one or more ......[2]. These are spread throughout the lattice and are said to be ......[3]. Because they can move about, the metal can conduct ......[4]. The forces between the metal ions in the lattice are very strong, so the ......[5] of metals are high.

Non-metal elements on the right-hand side of the Periodic Table exist as simple ......[6]. The forces between separate molecules (......[7] forces) are very weak and, as a consequence, these non-metals have low ......[8].

Non-metal elements in the centre of the Periodic Table (e.g. carbon and silicon) form ......[9] lattices. Here, each atom of the element is ......[10] bonded to its neighbour. The bonding between atoms (......[11] bonds) is therefore very strong and the elements have very high ......[12]. There are no free ......[13], so they do not conduct electricity. An exception to this is ......[14], the structure of which allows it to conduct electricity.   [½ mark each]

Total ☐
Maximum Total   7

Part B

(10 minutes)

Read the following passage and then answer the questions that follow.

A politician once said: 'There will be a time, I hope not far away, when it will be illegal to burn oil. In this Utopia, energy will be available, not from burning fossil fuels, but from other means that will be cheap, clean and safe. Oil will then be used efficiently for making organic chemical products that can be used over and over again for mankind.'

1. What is a fossil fuel? Give two further examples of types of fossil fuel besides oil. . . . . *wood coal* . . . . . . [3 marks]
2. Why do you think the politician thinks that oil is not 'cheap, clean and safe'? . . . . *drilling* . . . . [4 marks]
3. Give an example of a product that could be made from oil that can be 'used over and over again'. . . . . [1 mark]
4. Give the name of one of the main groups of chemicals that make up oil. . . . . [1 mark]
5. What are the products of burning the type of chemical you named in 4? . . . . [2 marks]

Total ☐
Maximum Total 11

Part C

(30 minutes)

Multiple choice questions [1 mark each]

1. How many neutrons are there in the nucleus of $^{23}_{11}Na$?
   A 10
   B 11
   C 12
   D 23
   E 34.

2. The decomposition of hydrogen peroxide is in accordance with the following equation:

$$2H_2O_2(l) \rightarrow 2H_2O(l) + O_2(g)$$

The rate of decomposition could *not* be determined by
   A measuring the volume of oxygen evolved
   B measuring the loss in mass of the reaction mixture in the vessel
   C measuring the mass of gas evolved
   D measuring the change in colour of the reaction
   E counting the number of bubbles of gas formed in a certain time interval.

3. Which of the following contains the same number of atoms as 6 g magnesium ($Mg = 24$; $Al = 27$; $Fe = 56$; $Ca = 40$; $S = 32$; $P = 31$)?
A 2.7 g aluminium
B 56 g iron
C 10 g calcium
D 6.4 g sulphur
E 6 g phosphorus.

4. The electronic configuration of the ion formed by sodium (atomic number 11) is
A 2, 8, 1
B 2, 8, 2
C 2, 7
D 2, 8
E 2, 9.

5. The catalyst used in the Contact process for the manufacture of sulphuric acid is
A iron
B manganese dioxide (manganese(IV) oxide)
C vanadium pentoxide
D copper sulphate
E none of these.

6. When aqueous sodium chloride is electrolysed using platinum electrodes
A hydrogen is evolved at the anode
B hydrogen is evolved at the cathode
C oxygen is evolved at the anode
D chlorine is evolved at the cathode
E sodium is formed at the cathode.

7. Methane burns in oxygen according to the equation
$$CH_4(g) + 2O_2(g) \rightarrow CO_2(g) + H_2O(l)$$
What volume of carbon dioxide will be formed when 15 cm^3 of methane burns in excess oxygen (measured at the same temperature and pressure)?
A 10 cm^3
B 15 cm^3
C 20 cm^3
D 25 cm^3
E 30 cm^3.

8. Atoms containing the same number of protons but differing numbers of neutrons are called
   A allotropes
   B isomers
   C atoms
   D isotopes
   E polymorphs.

9. Which of the following conducts electricity?
   A solid sugar
   B molten sugar
   C aqueous potassium nitrate
   D solid potassium nitrate
   E molten sulphur.

Questions 10–13 concern the following compounds:
   A methane
   B ethane
   C ethene
   D ethanol
   E poly(ethene).

10. Which contains a double bond?

11. Which contains only one carbon atom?

12. Which is the product of fermentation?

13. Which one is a solid at room temperature?

14. If a soil is acidic, it is best treated with
   A ammonium sulphate
   B calcium phosphate
   C calcium oxide
   D urea
   E water.

15. Which of the following statements about the halogens (group VII) is *incorrect*?
   A they form negative ions
   B their chemical reactivity with metals increases with atomic number
   C they can form both ionic and covalent compounds
   D the melting points increase with atomic number
   E the size of the atoms increases with atomic number

16. Which of the following gases will turn damp litmus paper blue?
    A steam
    B ammonia
    C hydrogen chloride
    D sulphur dioxide
    E carbon dioxide.

17. Metals *always*
    A have high melting points
    B burn in oxygen to form solid oxides
    C conduct electricity at room temperature
    D are hard and brittle
    E react with water to give alkaline solutions.

18. Sodium hydroxide solution is added to a solution of a compound of a metal. A green jelly-like precipitate is formed. The compound could have been
    A copper sulphate
    B iron(II) sulphate
    C copper nitrate
    D iron(III) nitrate
    E zinc nitrate.

19. Which of the following gases is most likely to be the cause of acid rain?
    A carbon dioxide
    B ammonia
    C sulphur dioxide
    D oxygen
    E argon.

20. Salts are *always*
    A soluble in water
    B electrolytes when molten
    C colourless
    D made by reacting an acid with an alkali
    E composed of two elements.

Total ☐
Maximum Total 20

Part D

(30 minutes)

Structured questions

1. What words or symbols should be placed in the boxes (a)–(e)
   below? .... [1 mark each]

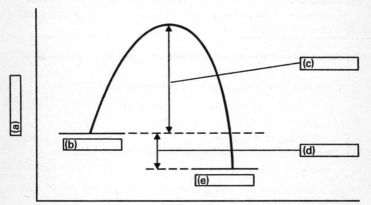

   Is the reaction endothermic or exothermic?   .... [1 mark]

2. The following table gives the physical properties of some elements:

Element	Magnetic	Electrical conductor	Density $(g\,cm^{-3})$	pH of solution of oxide of element
A	No	Yes	2.26	6
B	Yes	Yes	7.86	Insoluble
C	No	No	2.07	4
D	No	Yes	0.97	13
E	No	No	Very small	5
F	No	Yes	2.7	Insoluble

From the list, select an element (which may be used once, more than
once, or not at all) that
(a) is probably a gas   .... [1 mark]
(b) would float on water   .... [1 mark]

(c) has both metallic and non-metallic properties   . . . . . [1 mark]
(d) is certainly a metal   . . . . [1 mark]
(e) forms a basic oxide   . . . . [1 mark]
(f) forms an acidic oxide   . . . . [1 mark]
(g) would form an ionic compound with element E.   . . . . [1 mark]

3. Water in some areas of the country is said to be 'hard'.
(a) Name one compound that commonly causes hardness in water.
. . . . [1 mark]
(b) What is the effect of hard water on soap?
. . . . scum . . . . [1 mark]
(c) What is the effect of hard water on a soapless detergent?
. . . . lather . . . . [1 mark]
(d) Give two disadvantages of hard water compared to soft water.
. . . . . salts from rocks . . . . [2 marks]

Hardness can be removed by using an ion-exchange column.
(e) **What is meant by 'ion exchange'?**   . . . . [1 mark]
(f) Describe briefly how an ion-exchange column works.
. . . . [2 marks]

Nitric acid is sometimes added to the water supply of a greenhouse to clear the pipes of scale.
(g) **What is 'scale'?**   . . . . [1 mark]
(h) How does nitric acid remove the scale?
. . . . [2 marks]
(i) What is the other advantage of adding nitric acid?
. . . . [1 mark]

Total ☐
Maximum Total   25

Answers to Revision Test 4

Part A

1. three; 2. electrons; 3. delocalized (or free); 4. electricity;
5. melting points; 6. molecules; 7. intermolecular; 8. melting points;
9. three-dimensional; 10. covalently; 11. covalent; 12. melting points;
13. electrons; 14. graphite.

Part B

1. A fossil fuel is a fuel formed from living matter; coal and wood.
2. High costs are involved in its recovery from the earth and in refining; oil contains impurities; impurities cause pollution.
3. Plastics (e.g. poly(ethene)).
4. Alkanes.
5. Carbon dioxide and water.

Part C

1. C (11 protons, 12 neutrons)
2. D (the reactants and products are colourless)
3. C (6 g Mg is 0.25 mole)
4. D (Na loses its outer electron to become Na^+)
5. C
6. B (aqueous solution gives hydrogen at cathode and chlorine at anode)
7. B (equal number of moles, therefore same volume)
8. D
9. C (an electrolyte)
10. C (an alkene)
11. A
12. D
13. E (all polymers are solids)
14. C (a substance that is alkaline in solution)
15. B (they become less reactive down the group)
16. B
17. C
18. B (iron(III) compounds give a brown precipitate)
19. C (the only acidic gas in the list)
20. B (they are ionic; metal carbonates and sulphates contain three elements)

Part D

1. (a) Energy
   (b) Reactants
   (c) Activation energy
   (d) Heat change (or enthalpy change)

(e) Products.
The reaction is exothermic, because the products have less energy than the reactants.

2. (a) E (small density)
   (b) D (density less than one)
   (c) A (it is a conductor but the oxide is acidic)
   (d) B (conductor, magnetic, high density)
   (e) D (pH of solution greater than 7)
   (f) C or E (pH of solution less than 7)
   (g) D (E is a non-metal and therefore we require a metal)

   (a) Any calcium compound (e.g. calcium sulphate).
   (b) It forms an insoluble solid 'scum'.
   (c) None.
   (d) Washing requires more soap; scale (fur) forms in kettles and pipes.
   (e) Sodium ions are exchanged for calcium ions in the water.
   (f) Water is passed through a column packed with a resin containing sodium ions. These exchange with the calcium ions in the water, making it soft.
   (g) Calcium carbonate.
   (h) It reacts with it to form soluble calcium nitrate, carbon dioxide and water.
   (i) Calcium nitrate is a nitrogen-containing fertilizer.

Score for Revision Test 4

Part A	☐ 7
Part B	☐ 11
Part C	☐ 20
Part D	☐ 25
Total	☐ 63

☐ %

Revision Test 5

All syllabus topics

Part A

(10 minutes)

Fill in the missing words.

Nitrogen is a very important element. It is essential to all living things. The air contains about . . 7.5 . .[1]% nitrogen in the form of . 0.1.9 .[2]. This form of nitrogen, however, is not useful to living things because it is too . . . . . .[3]. A plant needs nitrogen in the form of its . . . . . .[4] and these are often added to soils as fertilizers.

A common fertilizer is ammonium nitrate. This is made by reacting ammonia with . . . . . .[5]. Ammonia is manufactured in the . . . . . .[6] process by mixing together . . . . . .[7] and . . . . . .[8] with a . . . . . .[9]. Ammonia is rarely added to soils because it is . . . . . .[10] and will kill the plants if used in excess.

Plants need other elements, and compounds containing . . . . . .[11] and . . . . . .[12] are often added to soils by farmers. A disadvantage in the use of fertilizers is that they can get into the . . . . . .[13] supply and cause . . . . . .[14]. [½ mark each]

Total   ☐

Maximum Total   7

Part B

(10 minutes)

Read the following passage and then answer the questions that follow.

When oxalic acid and concentrated sulphuric acid are mixed, the oxalic acid (a white solid) is dehydrated and both carbon monoxide and carbon dioxide are evolved. The following apparatus can be used for the preparation of carbon monoxide:

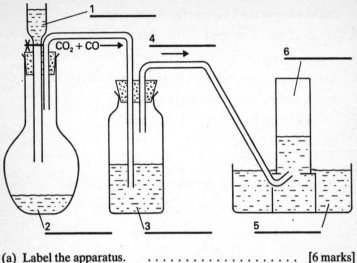

(a) Label the apparatus. .... [6 marks]
(b) What simple test could you use to show that carbon monoxide, and not carbon dioxide, had been prepared? .... [2 marks]
(c) Explain briefly why carbon monoxide is poisonous.

.... [1 mark]

Total ☐
Maximum Total 9

Part C

(30 minutes)

Multiple choice questions [1 mark each]

Questions 1–10 concern the following section of the Periodic Table. The letters do not represent the symbols of the elements.

I	II	III	IV	V	VI	VII	VIII
	C		D				A
B						E	

1. Which element has a full outer shell of electrons?

2. Which element is the most reactive metal?

3. Which element forms a covalent compound with element E?

4. Which element does not easily form any compounds?

5. Which element forms ions with charge 2+?

6. Which element has the lowest boiling point?

7. Which element is a green gas?

8. Which element is a low-melting-point metal?

9. Which element is a non-metal that conducts electricity?

10. Which element burns with a bright orange flame?

Questions 11–15 concern the following types of reactions found in organic chemistry:
    A polymerization
    B cracking
    C fermentation
    D addition
    E combustion.

Of which of these reactions are the following examples:

11. the formation of a high-melting-point solid from ethene?

12. the formation of two hydrocarbons with low boiling points from one hydrocarbon with a higher boiling point?

13. the decolorization of bromine water when it is mixed with ethene?

14. the formation of carbon dioxide and ethanol from glucose?

15. the formation of carbon dioxide and water from ethane?

16. 1.68 g of an oxide of chromium contains 1.04 g of chromium. What is the formula of this oxide ($Cr = 52$; $O = 16$)?
    A Cr_2O
    B CrO
    C Cr_2O_3
    D CrO_2
    E Cr_2O_5.

17. If a neutral atom has 16 electrons and 16 neutrons its mass number (nucleon number) will be

A 10
B 15
C 16
D 20
E 32.

18. Reactive metals are extracted by

A displacement (reduction) with carbon
B electrolysis of their aqueous salts
C electrolysis of their molten compounds
D heating one of their compounds in air
E electrolysis of their solid compounds.

19. Sodium hydrogencarbonate decomposes according to the following equation:

$$2NaHCO_3 \rightarrow Na_2CO_3 + H_2O + CO_2$$

What mass of sodium carbonate (Na_2CO_3) is produced when 4.2 g of sodium hydrogencarbonate undergo complete decomposition ($Na = 23$; $O = 16$; $H = 1$; $C = 12$)?

A 1.33 g
B 2.1 g
C 2.65 g
D 4.2 g
E 5.3 g.

20. Which of the following statements is correct?
A both graphite and diamond conduct electricity
B the atoms in graphite are arranged tetrahedrally
C graphite and diamond are isotopes of carbon
D graphite and diamond burn in oxygen to form carbon dioxide
E diamond is less dense than graphite.

Total ☐
Maximum Total 20

Part D

(30 minutes)

Structured questions

1. The apparatus shown below was set up to investigate the composition of air.

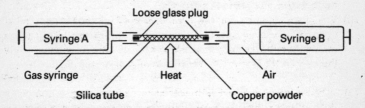

Air is passed from one syringe to the other while the copper is heated. Oxygen in the air reacts with the copper.

(a) What would you see happening to the copper during the experiment. Write an equation for the change.   . . . . [2 marks]

(b) What is the purpose of the loose glass plugs in the silica tubes?
. . . . [1 mark]

The initial readings on the syringes were
   Syringe A: $50 \, cm^3$
   Syringe B: $25 \, cm^3$

After passing the air over the heated copper for a few minutes, the apparatus was allowed to cool, and the volumes in the syringes read again. The readings were

   Syringe A: $0 \, cm^3$
   Syringe B: $60 \, cm^3$

(c) Why was the apparatus allowed to cool before measuring the final volume?   . . . . [1 mark]

(d) Explain why the volume of air decreases during the experiment.
. . . . [1 mark]

(e) Calculate this reduction in volume.   . . . . [1 mark]

(f) From the value you have calculated in (e) and the original volume of air used, calculate the percentage (by volume) of oxygen in the air.   . . . . [2 marks]

(g) Give the names of two other gases commonly found in air.

.... [2 marks]

2. Ethanol (C_2H_5OH) is produced in large quantities by the action of yeast on a sugar (e.g. glucose).

(a) What is the name of the process by which ethanol is produced from glucose? What method would you choose to separate ethanol from the reaction mixture in this process? .... [2 marks]

(b) Write an equation for the combustion of ethanol in air. What volume (measured at room temperature and pressure) of carbon dioxide would be produced when 4.6 g of ethanol is completely burnt ($C = 12$; $H = 1$; $O = 16$; 1 mole of gas occupies 24 dm^3)?

.... [5 marks]

(c) When ethanol is mixed with potassium dichromate solution and a drop of concentrated sulphuric acid is added to acidify the mixture, the ethanol is oxidized.

  (i) What would you *see* happening to the reaction mixture?

.... [1 mark]

  (ii) What is the *organic* product in this reaction?

.... [1 mark]

  (iii) What simple test would you choose to confirm your answer in (ii)? .... [1 mark]

3. Use the metals from the following list to answer the questions below:

sodium potassium copper zinc magnesium iron silver calcium

(a) Arrange the metals listed above in order of reactivity, the most reactive first. .... [2 marks]

(b) Give the name of one metal which would react with cold dilute hydrochloric acid, but *not* with cold water. Write an equation for its reaction with acid. .... [2 marks]

(c) Give the name of one metal which would probably catch fire if added to water. Write an equation for this reaction.

.... [2 marks]

(d) Give the name of one metal which readily forms an oxide that could be reduced back to the metal with hydrogen gas. Write an equation for the reaction of the oxide with hydrogen.

.... [2 marks]

(e) An iron nail is placed in a solution of copper sulphate.

  (i) What would you observe happening? .... [1 mark]

    (ii) Write an ionic equation for the change that is occurring?

. . . . [1 mark]

    (iii) Is the reaction endothermic or exothermic?

. . . . [1 mark]

Total ☐

Maximum Total 31

Answers to Revision Test 5

Part A

1. 80; 2. nitrogen gas (or N_2 molecules); 3. inert (or unreactive);
4. compounds; 5. nitric acid; 6. Haber; 7. nitrogen; 8. hydrogen;
9. catalyst; 10. alkaline; 11. potassium; 12. phosphorus; 13. water;
14. pollution.

Part B

(a) 1. Concentrated sulphuric acid
    2. Oxalic acid.
    3. Potassium (or sodium) hydroxide
    4. Carbon monoxide
    5. Water
    6. Carbon monoxide.
(b) Test to see if it burns in air: CO burns with blue flame; CO_2 does not burn.
(c) It reacts with haemoglobin in the red blood cells, thereby excluding oxygen.

Part C

1. A (noble gas)
2. B (alkali metal)
3. D (group IV)
4. A (noble gas)
5. C (group II metal with two outer electrons)
6. A
7. E (chlorine)

8. B (alkali metal)
9. D (carbon graphite)
10. B (sodium)
11. A (poly(ethene) formed)
12. B
13. D (test for unsaturation, i.e. double bonds)
14. C
15. E
16. D (0.02 mole of Cr (1.04/52) and 0.4 mole of O ((1.68 − 1.04)/16))
17. E (16 electrons, therefore 16 protons)
18. C (aqueous compounds will give hydrogen)
19. C (0.05 mole of $NaHCO_3$, therefore 0.025 mole of Na_2CO_3 formed)
20. D (allotropes have identical *chemical* properties)

Part D

1. (a) The copper would turn from brown to black:
       $2Cu + O_2 \rightarrow 2CuO$.
   (b) To prevent the copper powder passing into the syringes, but allowing gas to flow.
   (c) Gas expands when hot; readings must be taken at the same temperature for comparison of volumes.
   (d) Oxygen is removed from the air as it reacts with the copper.
   (e) $(50 + 25) − (0 + 60) = 15 \text{ cm}^3$.
   (f) Original volume $= 75 \text{ cm}^3$; volume of oxygen $= 15 \text{ cm}^3$.
       % oxygen $= 15/75 \times 100 = 20\%$.
   (g) Carbon dioxide and nitrogen.

2. (a) Fermentation; distillation (or fractional distillation).
   (b) $2C_2H_5OH + 7O_2 \rightarrow 4CO_2 + 6H_2O$.
       4.6 g ethanol $= 4.6/46 = 0.1$ mole.
       Therefore 2×0.1 mole of CO_2 is produced.
       That is $0.2 \times 24 = 4.8 \text{ dm}^3$ of CO_2 are produced.
   (c) (i) The solution turns green from orange.
       (ii) Ethanoic acid.
      (iii) Smell it (it has a vinegary smell).

3. (a) Potassium, sodium, calcium, magnesium, zinc, iron, copper, silver.

3. (a) Potassium, sodium, calcium, magnesium, zinc, iron, copper, silver.

   (b) Zinc or magnesium:
   $$Zn + 2HCl \rightarrow ZnCl_2 + H_2.$$

   (c) Sodium or potassium:
   $$Na + H_2O \rightarrow NaOH + \tfrac{1}{2}H_2.$$

   (d) Copper:
   $$CuO + H_2 \rightarrow Cu + H_2O.$$

   (e) (i) Brown solid forms on nail and solution becomes colourless.
      (ii) $Fe + Cu^{2+} \rightarrow Fe^{2+} + Cu.$
      (iii) Exothermic.

Score for Revision Test 5

Part A	☐ 7
Part B	☐ 9
Part C	☐ 20
Part D	☐ 31
Total	☐ 67

☐ %

Multiple Choice Revision Test 1

Twenty multiple choice questions on the whole syllabus

(30 minutes)

Questions 1–5 concern the following practical techniques:
  A chromatography
  B distillation
  C crystallization
  D filtration
  E centrifugation.

Which technique would best be used to
1. isolate solid copper sulphate from an aqueous solution?

2. separate the dyes in coloured sweets?

3. obtain water from ink?

4. remove solid ground coffee powder from a cup of coffee?

5. separate diesel oil from crude oil?

6. Which of the following shows the metals in the correct order of reactivity (most reactive first)?
  A copper sodium silver lead
  B sodium lead copper silver
  C silver copper lead sodium
  D lead sodium copper silver
  E sodium copper lead silver.

7. The following table gives the colours of three indicators in strongly acidic and strongly alkaline solutions and the pH at which the colour changes.

Indicator	Colour in strong acid	pH of colour change	Colour in strong alkali
Phenolphthalein	Colourless	9	Pink
Methyl red	Red	5	Yellow
Methyl orange	Red	3	Yellow

If each indicator is put, in turn, into dilute hydrochloric acid of pH 4, what colour would they have?

	Phenolphthalein	Methyl red	Methyl orange
A	colourless	yellow	red
B	colourless	red	yellow
C	colourless	yellow	yellow
D	pink	red	yellow
E	pink	yellow	red

Questions 8–12 concern the following gases found in air:
  A oxygen
  B nitrogen
  C argon
  D carbon dioxide
  E water vapour.

8. Which reacts with sulphur to give a gaseous product?

9. Which has the highest boiling point?

10. Which is the least reactive?

11. Which gas reacts to form compounds which find uses as fertilizers?

12. Which gas is present in air in the lowest concentration?

13. Which of the following compounds contains the greatest percentage by mass of nitrogen ($N = 14$; $H = 1$; $Cl = 35.5$; $O = 16$; $S = 32$; $C = 12$)?
  A NH_3
  B NH_4Cl
  C NH_4NO_3
  D $(NH_4)_2SO_4$
  E $CO(NH_2)_2$.

14. A compound X rapidly decolorizes bromine water in the absence of light. This indicates that X is
  A an alkane
  B an ester
  C saturated
  D unsaturated
  E organic.

15. The diagram below shows an energy profile for the reaction between hydrogen and oxygen to produce water.

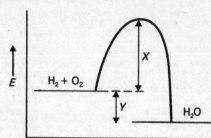

Which of the following is *incorrect*?
   A X is the heat change in the reaction
   B heat is evolved in the reaction
   C energy is required to start the reaction
   D the products have less energy than the reactants
   E the reaction is exothermic.

16. Which of the following oxides is/are acidic?
   1 nitrogen oxide (NO)
   2 carbon dioxide (CO_2)
   3 calcium oxide (CaO)
   4 sulphur dioxide (SO_2)
   A 1, 2, 3   B 1, 2   C 2, 4   D 4   E other.

17. Rubidium is below potassium in group I. It is likely to
   1 form 1+ ions
   2 form an insoluble hydroxide
   3 form a soluble nitrate
   4 have a lower melting point than potassium
   A 1, 2, 3   B 1, 3   C 2, 4   D 4   E other.

18. What is the fomula of the compound formed between element Q (electronic configuration 2, 8, 1) and element R (electronic configuration 2, 8, 6)?
   A QR
   B QR_2
   C Q_2R
   D Q_2R_3
   E QR_3.

19. Which one of the following species is the cause of acidity in an aqueous solution?

   A H_2O

   B H_3O^+

   C H^-

   D OH^-

   E HCl.

20. The atoms of a certain element contain 9 electrons. This element will

   A form positive ions

   B be unreactive

   C form negative ions

   D be a metal

   E conduct electricity.

Answers to Multiple Choice Revision Test 1

1. C (solid crystals are required, distillation not suitable)

2. A

3. B (boiling ink gives water vapour which can be condensed)

4. D (this is what happens in a coffee filter machine; centrifugation would work, but filtration is easier and more straightforward)

5. B

6. B (the most reactive has to be sodium, then choose between B and E)

7. B (methyl orange changes from red to yellow at pH 3; it will be yellow at pH 4)

8. A (sulphur dioxide)

9. E (the others are all gases at room temperature)

10. C (noble gas)

11. B (ammonium compounds and nitrates)

12. D (0.03%)

13. A (calculate the relative molecular mass for each; divide this into the mass of nitrogen in 1 mole; for ammonia, 1 mole of ammonia (17 g) contains 14 g nitrogen, a percentage of 82%; the question could also be done by inspection – ammonia is by far the richest in nitrogen)

14. **D** (bromine reacts with unsaturated compounds that have carbon to carbon double bonds in an addition reaction; saturated compounds (e.g. alkanes) only react in the presence of light)
15. **A** (X is the activation energy)
16. **C** ((nitrogen oxide is neutral)
17. **E** (1, 3 and 4)
18. **C** (first element is in group I forming 1+ ions, second is in group VI forming 2− ions)
19. **B** (hydrated H^+ ions, oxonium ions)
20. **C** (9 electrons, therefore electronic configuration 2, 7, therefore group VII)

Score

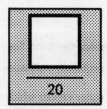

20

Multiple Choice Revision Test 2

Twenty multiple choice questions on the whole syllabus

(30 minutes)

The following is a list of metals:
   A sodium
   B calcium
   C copper
   D aluminium
   E silver.

Choose, from metals A–E, the metal which
1. is found free in nature.

2. has the lowest melting point.

3. will react readily with cold water.

4. forms a chloride, the solution of which is blue.

5. forms positive ions the most easily.

6. 100 g of powdered calcium carbonate (an excess) is added to dilute hydrochloric acid of pH 2. What will be the pH after the addition of the carbonate?
   A 2
   B 5
   C 7
   D 9
   E 12.

7. How many moles of nitrogen atoms contain the same number of atoms as 48 g of oxygen atoms (N = 14; O = 16)?
   A 1
   B 2
   C 3
   D 4
   E 5.

8. The compound

$$H-\underset{\underset{H}{|}}{\overset{\overset{H}{|}}{C}}-C\overset{O}{\underset{OH}{\diagdown}}$$

is an example of
   A an alcohol
   B a carboxylic acid
   C a mineral acid
   D an alkane
   E an ester.

9. Which one of the following metals is extracted from its oxide using electrolysis?
   A copper
   B iron
   C aluminium
   D silver
   E lead.

10. When decane ($C_{10}H_{22}$) is cracked, which of the following could be among the products?
   1 C_2H_6
   2 C_2H_4
   3 C_4H_6
   4 $C_{12}H_{26}$
   A 1, 2, 3   B 1, 3   C 2, 4   D 4   E other.

11. If the nucleus $^{231}_{90}$Th emits an alpha particle, the mass number (nucleon number) of the remaining nucleus will be
   A 88
   B 90
   C 141
   D 229
   E 227.

12. The mass in grams of 1 mole of aluminium sulphate ($Al_2(SO_4)_3$) is ($Al = 27$; $S = 32$; $O = 16$)
   A 246
   B 267
   C 294
   D 315
   E 342.

13. Which of the following processes is strongly exothermic?
  A the boiling of water
  B the production of starch by a green leaf
  C the sparking of a mixture of hydrogen and oxygen
  D the rusting of iron
  E the further dilution of a dilute acid.

14. Which of the following gases is colourless, insoluble in water and turns hot black copper oxide red-brown?
  A carbon dioxide
  B water vapour
  C hydrogen
  D chlorine
  E oxygen.

15. A catalyst is substance that
  A stops a reaction
  B starts a reaction
  C speeds up a reaction by increasing the concentration of the reactants
  D speeds up a reaction but remains chemically unchanged at the end of the reaction
  E takes in the heat of the reaction.

16. When chloroethene

$$\begin{array}{cc} H & H \\ \diagdown & \diagup \\ C{=}C \\ \diagup & \diagdown \\ H & Cl \end{array}$$

is polymerized, the polymer has the structure (n denotes a large number)

A $\left(\begin{array}{cccc} H & H & H & H \\ | & | & | & | \\ C-C-C-C \\ | & | & | & | \\ Cl & Cl & Cl & Cl \end{array}\right)_n$

B $\left(\begin{array}{cccc} Cl & Cl & Cl & Cl \\ | & | & | & | \\ C-C-C-C \\ | & | & | & | \\ Cl & Cl & Cl & Cl \end{array}\right)_n$

C $\left(\begin{array}{cccc} \overset{\displaystyle H}{\underset{\displaystyle |}{|}} & \overset{\displaystyle H}{\underset{\displaystyle |}{|}} & \overset{\displaystyle H}{\underset{\displaystyle |}{|}} & \overset{\displaystyle H}{\underset{\displaystyle |}{|}} \\ -C & -C & -C & -C- \\ \overset{\displaystyle |}{H} & \overset{\displaystyle |}{H} & \overset{\displaystyle |}{H} & \overset{\displaystyle |}{H} \end{array}\right)_n$

D $\left(\begin{array}{cccc} H & H & H & H \\ -C & -C & -C & -C- \\ H & Cl & Cl & Cl \end{array}\right)_n$

E $\left(\begin{array}{cccc} H & H & H & H \\ -C & -C & -C & -C- \\ H & Cl & H & Cl \end{array}\right)_n .$

17. What volume of carbon dioxide is produced (measured under the same conditions) when $10\,cm^3$ of ethane undergoes complete combustion?

   A $10\,cm^3$
   B $20\,cm^3$
   C $30\,cm^3$
   D $40\,cm^3$
   E $50\,cm^3$.

18. In the reaction between hydrochloric acid and sodium thiosulphate solution, sulphur forms as a cloudy precipitate. The rate of the reaction can be investigated by measuring the time it takes for the cloudiness to obscure a mark on the reaction vessel base. This time is

   A equal to the rate of reaction
   B proportional to the rate of reaction
   C inversely proportional to the rate of reaction
   D independent of the rate of reaction
   E proportional to the rate of reaction squared.

19. Zinc reacts with hydrochloric acid according to the equation

$$Zn(s) + 2HCl(aq) \rightarrow ZnCl_2(aq) + H_2(g)$$

The volume (in dm^3) of hydrogen produced (measured at room temperature and pressure) when 0.1 mole of zinc reacts is

   A 1.2
   B 2.4

C 0.6

D 0.3

E 0.15.

20. The catalyst used in the Contact process for the manufacture of sulphuric acid is

A iron

B manganese dioxide

C vanadium pentoxide

D copper sulphate

E none of these.

Answers to Multiple Choice Revision Test 2

1. E (the most unreactive)
2. A (group I)
3. A (group I)
4. C (transition metal, therefore coloured compounds)
5. A (group I)
6. C (excess, so carbonate fully neutralizes the acid)
7. C ($48\,g = 48/16$ moles of atoms of oxygen)
8. B (ethanoic acid)
9. C (the most reactive)
10. A (any smaller-chain alkane or alkene)
11. E (alpha particles have a mass number of 4)
12. E
13. C (explosive)
14. C (copper oxide + hydrogen $\rightarrow$ copper (red-brown) + water)
15. D
16. E
17. B (ethane is C_2H_6; 1 mole of ethane produces 2 mole of carbon dioxide; therefore $10\,cm^3$ produces $20\,cm^3$)
18. C (fast (high) rate means that the mark is covered up in a short (low) time)
19. B (0.1 mole of zinc produces 0.1 mole of hydrogen, which occupies $0.1 \times 24\,dm^3$)
20. C

Score

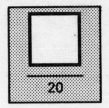

Multiple Choice Revision Test 3

Twenty multiple choice questions on the whole syllabus

(30 minutes)

Questions 1–5: select the letter that corresponds to the section in the Periodic Table shown below.

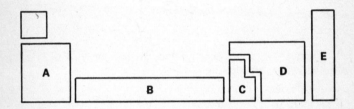

1. Metals in this section often form more than one compound with another element.

2. Metals in this section are very reactive, often burning in air with coloured flames.

3. Because the gases in this section are so unreactive, they were only discovered this century.

4. The element with electronic configuration 2, 8, 7 is found in this section.

5. The only coloured liquid element is found in this section.

6. Which two elements are combined in petrol?

    A carbon and hydrogen
    B carbon and oxygen
    C sulphur and hydrogen
    D sulphur and oxygen
    E carbon and sulphur.

7. Which of the following could be used as a fertilizer?
   A sodium chloride
   B sulphuric acid
   C ammonium sulphate
   D sodium sulphate
   E hydrochloric acid.

8. Household bleach would be expected to have a pH of
   A 1
   B 5
   C 7
   D 9
   E 14.

9. When aqueous potassium chloride is electrolysed with graphite electrodes, the products are

	Cathode	Anode
A	oxygen	chlorine
B	potassium	oxygen
C	potassium	chlorine
D	hydrogen	chlorine
E	hydrogen	oxygen.

10. Metal R can displace metal Q from a solution of the nitrate of Q. Metal P is extracted from its oxide by heating with carbon, but metal Q can only be extracted by electrolysing the molten oxide of Q. What is the order of reactivity of these three metals (the most reactive first)?
   A P Q R
   B R P Q
   C R Q P
   D P R Q
   E Q R P.

11. Which of the following elements exist as diatomic molecules under normal conditions?
   1 magnesium
   2 chlorine
   3 argon
   4 oxygen
   A 1, 2, 3   B 1, 3   C 2, 4   D 4   E other.

12. If a reaction is endothermic, then
   A the reaction is very slow
   B more energy is required to break the bonds of the reactants than is released by forming the bonds of the product
   C the energy of the reactants is less than the energy of the products
   D more energy is given off towards the end of the reaction
   E energy is not required to start the reaction.

13. Which one of the following elements burns in air to give an oxide that dissolves in water to give a solution of pH 11?
   A sulphur
   B copper
   C sodium
   D hydrogen
   E iron.

14. Which one of the following metals will react with dilute hydrochloric acid but *not* with cold water?
   A sodium
   B magnesium
   C copper
   D potassium
   E lead.

15. Chlorine will form an ionic compound with the element of electronic configuration
   A 2, 7
   B 2, 6
   C 2, 5
   D 2, 8, 1
   E 2, 8, 6.

16. An element burns in oxygen with an orange flame. The oxide that forms readily dissolves in water to form a solution with pH of 11. The element is
   A sulphur
   B silicon
   C carbon
   D sodium
   E calcium.

17. In the extraction of aluminium from bauxite (aluminium oxide), electrodes are made of carbon. The anode needs frequent replacement because
    A it conducts electricity for short periods only
    B it becomes coated with aluminium and ceases to work
    C it reacts with the oxygen gas that is formed
    D it melts during electrolysis
    E it reacts with the aluminium that is formed.

18. If a catalyst is poisoned,
    A it is broken into smaller peices
    B it becomes more effective
    C it is activated
    D the reaction slows down
    E the reaction speeds up.

19. Which of the following properties is/are shown by all of the group I metals?
    1 all form ions with 1+ charge
    2 all have low melting points compared with other metals
    3 all have low densities
    4 all form coloured compounds
    A 1, 2, 3   B 1, 3   C 2, 4   D 4   E other.

20. A beta particle has
    A a positive charge and negligible mass
    B a negative charge and negligible mass
    C no charge and negligible mass
    D a positive charge and a mass of 1 unit
    E a negative charge and a mass of 1 unit.

Answers to Multiple Choice Revision Test 3

1. B (transition metals)
2. A (alkali metals, group I)
3. E (noble gases, group VIII)
4. D (7 outer electrons, therefore group VII)
5. D (bromine)
6. A (petrol is a hydrocarbon)
7. C (contains nitrogen)

8. **B** (bleach is a solution of chlorine)
9. **D** (potassium is more reactive than hydrogen)
10. **C** (R is more reactive than Q; P is an unreactive metal because it can be extracted by displacement/reduction with carbon)
11. **C** (diatomic gases)
12. **B** (energy taken in by system)
13. **C** (alkaline, therefore metal; iron does not burn in air)
14. **B** (lead does not react with dilute acid)
15. **D** (1 outer electron, therefore a metal – sodium)
16. **D** (calcium burns with a red flame)
17. **C** (to form carbon dioxide gas which escapes)
18. **D** (catalyst made less effective)
19. **A** (transition metals form coloured compounds)
20. **B**

Score

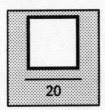

20

FOR THE BEST IN PAPERBACKS, LOOK FOR THE

In every corner of the world, on every subject under the sun, Penguin represents quality and variety – the very best in publishing today.

For complete information about books available from Penguin – including Pelicans, Puffins, Peregrines and Penguin Classics – and how to order them, write to us at the appropriate address below. Please note that for copyright reasons the selection of books varies from country to country.

In the United Kingdom: For a complete list of books available from Penguin in the U.K., please write to *Dept E.P., Penguin Books Ltd, Harmondsworth, Middlesex, UB7 0DA*

In the United States: For a complete list of books available from Penguin in the U.S., please write to *Dept BA, Penguin, 299 Murray Hill Parkway, East Rutherford, New Jersey 07073*

In Canada: For a complete list of books available from Penguin in Canada, please write to *Penguin Books Canada Ltd, 2801 John Street, Markham, Ontario L3R 1B4*

In Australia: For a complete list of books available from Penguin in Australia, please write to the *Marketing Department, Penguin Books Australia Ltd, P.O. Box 257, Ringwood, Victoria 3134*

In New Zealand: For a complete list of books available from Penguin in New Zealand, please write to the *Marketing Department, Penguin Books (NZ) Ltd, Private Bag, Takapuna, Auckland 9*

In India: For a complete list of books available from Penguin, please write to *Penguin Overseas Ltd, 706 Eros Apartments, 56 Nehru Place, New Delhi, 110019*

In Holland: For a complete list of books available from Penguin in Holland, please write to *Penguin Books Nederland B.V., Postbus 195, NL–1380AD Weesp, Netherlands*

In Germany: For a complete list of books available from Penguin, please write to *Penguin Books Ltd, Friedrichstrasse 10 – 12, D–6000 Frankfurt Main 1, Federal Republic of Germany*

In Spain: For a complete list of books available from Penguin in Spain, please write to *Longman Penguin España, Calle San Nicolas 15, E–28013 Madrid, Spain*

FOR THE BEST IN PAPERBACKS, LOOK FOR THE 🐧

PENGUIN MASTERSTUDIES AND CRITICAL STUDIES

This comprehensive list, designed for advanced level and first-year under-
graduate studies, includes:

SUBJECTS
Applied Mathematics
Biology
Drama: Text into Performance
Geography
Pure Mathematics

LITERATURE
Absalom and Achitophel
Barchester Towers
Dr Faustus
Eugénie Grandet
The Great Gatsby
Gulliver's Travels
Joseph Andrews
The Mill on the Floss
A Passage to India
Persuasion *and* Emma
Portrait of a Lady
Tender Is the Night
Vanity Fair
The Waste Land

CHAUCER
The Knight's Tale
The Miller's Tale
The Nun's Priest's Tale
The Pardoner's Tale
The Prologue to The Canterbury
  Tales
A Chaucer Handbook

SHAKESPEARE
Antony & Cleopatra
Hamlet
King Lear
Measure for Measure
Much Ado About Nothing
Othello
The Tempest
A Shakespeare Handbook